A Children's Book About

INTERRUPTING

Grolier Enterprises, Inc. offers a varied selection of children's
book racks and tote bags. For details on ordering, please write:
Grolier Enterprises Inc., Sherman Turnpike, Danbury, CT 06816
Attn: Premium Department

Managing Editor: Ellen Klarberg
Copy Editor: Annette Gooch
Editorial Assistant: Lana Eberhard
Art Director: Jennifer Wiezel
Production Artist: Gail Miller
Illustration Designer: Bartholomew
Inking Artist: Micah Schwaberow
Coloring Artist: Susie Hornig
Lettering Artist: Linda Hanney
Typographer: Communication Graphics

A Children's Book About

INTERRUPTING

By Joy Berry

GROLIER ENTERPRISES CORP.

This book is about Sam.

Reading about Sam can help you understand and deal with *interrupting.*

You are interrupting when you *do something that makes it difficult for people to concentrate.*

You are interrupting when you *do something that causes people to stop what they are doing.*

You are interrupting when you *talk when other people are talking.*

When someone interrupts you:
- How do you feel?
- What do you think?
- What do you do?

When someone interrupts you:
- You might feel frustrated and angry.
- You might think the person is not fun to be with.
- You might decide to stay away from the person.

Avoid interrupting people.

Try not to interrupt people who are *thinking or trying to do something.*

- Avoid talking to them.
- Do not make noises that would bother them.
- Do not do things that would distract them.

Try not to interrupt people who are *talking to you.*

- Allow them to finish talking before you speak.
- Say "excuse me" if you must interrupt them.

Try not to interrupt people who are *talking to each other.*

- Do not talk with them or listen to what they are saying unless they want you to join them.
- Do not get between people who are talking to each other.
- Say "excuse me" if you must interrupt people who are talking.

Try not to interrupt people who are *talking on the telephone.*

- Avoid talking to them.
- Do not do anything that would make it difficult for them to hear.
- Do not do anything that would make it difficult for them to concentrate.

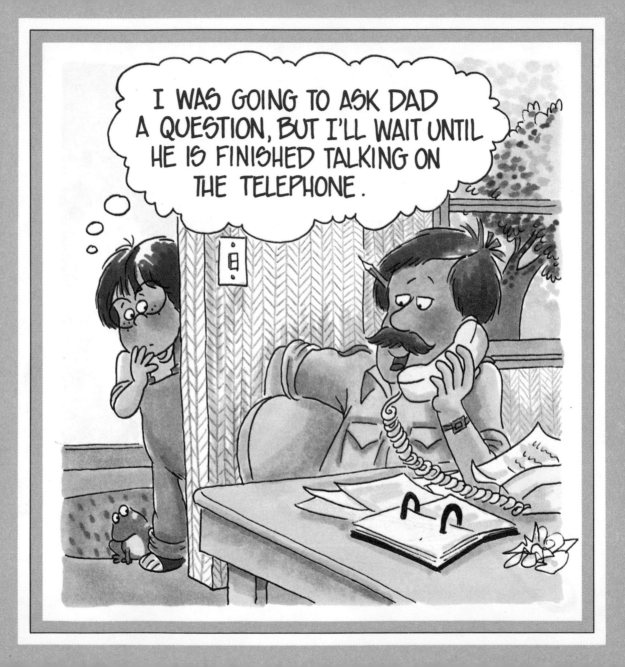

Do not interrupt people who are *listening to something or watching TV.*

- Do not talk to them.
- Do not make noises that would make it difficult for them to hear.
- Do not change channels on the TV unless they want you to.
- Do not put yourself between them and the TV.

Try not to interrupt people who are *watching a movie or a performance.*

- If you must pass in front of others to get to your seat, move quickly and quietly.
- Do not talk loudly or make other disturbing noises.
- If eating is permitted, eat neatly and quietly.
- Do not hit or kick the seat in front of you or beside you.
- If possible, stay seated until the movie or performance is over.

Try not to interrupt people who are *resting or sleeping.*

- If possible, stay away from them.
- Be as quiet as you can so that you will not disturb them.

It is important to treat people the way you want to be treated.

If you do not want people to interrupt you, you must not interrupt them.